*To* G·L·P·E·E

*Hartmut Aufderstraße*

# FALLEN
# INTO TIME

*Poeticized Thoughts*

Limitless thanks to my intrepid friend

TRACEY SCHAAL

for proofreading this book and her priceless traces

Mentions légales

© 2022 Hartmut Aufderstraße

Édition : BoD – Books on Demand,
12/14 rond-point des Champs-Élysées, 75008 Paris
Impression : BoD - Books on Demand, Norderstedt, Allemagne

Picture of the author, cover design: Jan Aufderstraße

ISBN : 978-2-3223-9181-3
Dépôt légal : Février 2022

# Contents

Fallen into Time .................................................. 9

Without the Least Idea ....................................... 10

The Book ............................................................ 11

Days .................................................................. 12

Thoughts ........................................................... 14

Ten Minutes Hardly ........................................... 15

Sometimes, Meditating ..................................... 16

Social Safety Net ............................................... 17

Fears ................................................................. 18

Colors Not Flying............................................... 20

Deseo ................................................................ 22

Desire................................................................ 24

Et altera pars..................................................... 26

The Other Side .................................................. 27

Borderland ........................................................ 28

That Morning When I Left ................................. 30

Excessive Dreamdefiant Exaggeration.................... 32

Mea Maxima Culpa............................................ 33

Storming Brain With Dictionary......................... 34

Vertigo .............................................................. 35

Land, Waste ...................................................... 36

- A Night's Speech .................................................. 37
- Negations .............................................................. 38
- Dreamless ............................................................. 40
- About the Memory of Soul ................................... 41
- Balancing Act ....................................................... 42
- Assistance ............................................................ 43
- Da Capo ................................................................ 44
- Nos acercamos así ............................................... 46
- The Way We Approached ..................................... 47
- What Will You Do? ................................................ 48
- Sin consecuencia ................................................. 50
- Without Consequence ......................................... 51
- Omissions ............................................................. 52
- Complicated Constructions ................................ 53
- Don't Be a Frog .................................................... 54
- When I Invented the Wheel ................................. 56
- When I Invented then the Powder ...................... 57
- When I Invented then the Rainbow .................... 58
- Infringing the Provisions .................................... 59
- Morpheus' Brother .............................................. 60
- Seems That's the Way I Am ................................ 62
- Curtain ................................................................. 63

- Doubts .................................................................. 64
- The Jump ............................................................. 66
- Roundabout ......................................................... 67
- Bugs ..................................................................... 68
- Tua Maxima Culpa ............................................... 70
- Paper .................................................................... 71
- Commandments of The Past ................................ 72
- Who I Would Have Loved to Be ........................... 74
- What I Would Have Liked to Be ........................... 75
- Two-Class Society ................................................ 76
- City Trips ............................................................. 77
- Notes for a Speech to Graduates ......................... 78
- Rhetorical Questions ........................................... 79
- Lifted Out of Time ............................................... 80
- Reading Certain Texts .......................................... 81
- Citations .............................................................. 82
- Postfarce .............................................................. 83
- About the Author ................................................. 84
- There Is Some Free Space Here ........................... 86

# Fallen into Time

Nobody wanted me

Or did, indeed?

A child of Love?

Who knows

I can't ask anyone anymore


Into Time I fell just out of Nothingness


And did arrive

# Without the Least Idea

Ashtray

Pipe

Its mouthpiece separated from the bowl

Glass with brass clips

Twenty-three in all

Candle, hole-punch, paper weight and piggy bank

Goblet filled with brushes, ball-points and erasers

One more ashtray and a pocketbook

Is this meaningful?

Why am I sitting here?

# The Book

Now finally I feel the power

Tomorrow I'll kick off

So far everything is yet prepared

Paper

Wastepaper basket, too

Tobacco, pipe and whiskey

Ideas are flowing steadily

Nothing easier to do

Than to write them down

I only need some peacefulness

And will tomorrow start my work


Or maybe the day after

# Days

There are these days when
A flower scribbled on paper will do
And days when
Hours are too few

There are these days with flashing lights
And days with children's songs

There are days filled with silence
And days with pizza orgies

Days exist
Reduced to quarters of an hour
Days with misunderstandings
But even misunderstanding
Is a form of understanding

There are these rainy days
And nights of heaven clear with frost
Magnificent to take a walk, but…

There are days of fairy tales
And days of poetry

Then there are so-called one-word-days

Days exist with sparkling wine
Or only sparkling water
Or much too much coffee

There are days of timid yes and no
Or a cheerful "NO"

Then days of anticipation

Days with 10 or 16 amperes
Or those
When fuses are not needed

# Thoughts

May thoughts be free
So what's the big deal?
Emotions are not


I think what I want
But what delights me
Comes out of the belly


And if I were locked
In the gloomy dungeon
Of my poor soul
Thoughts would not break down
To pieces the walls




*(Inspired by an old German freedom chant)*

# Ten Minutes Hardly

Ten minutes hardly may I
Be lost in my own suffering
It's either tele- or smartphone
The bell on the front door
Or from downstairs a voice that cries: "Coffee!"

The rush is not attainable
Nor happiness nor grief

It's melancholy only
You can act out intensely

# Sometimes, Meditating

Or unexpectedly

At a break in a sentence

My face may show

Imperceptibly

A smile

Not without reason

# Social Safety Net

In times of
Cyclical sentimental downturn
Higher spiritual incomes
Can absolutely be charged
With an interior
Additional levy

Until the trough
Has been passed

# Fears

Of a soul remaining child

Fear

Of being misunderstood
That certain texts may no longer be valid
Of masks (my own ones, too)
Of too much public
Of getting too close
Of hurting

Of losing spontaneousness
That my mediocrity might be realized
That solidarity, basic consensus and trust
May be damaged

That not everything is said
That too much could have been said
To get false impressions
Not to recognize coherencies

Okay – let's admit:

Fear

Not to be liked anymore

*But I'm just a soul whose intentions are good*
*Oh Lord, don't let me be misunderstood*

Don't get to miss our next episode
Entitled "Confidence"

# Colors Not Flying

Not with flying colors
Not with waving skirts

With careful steps

Not with vehemence
Nor full force

Slowly, all by yourself

Not with burning gaze
Nor effervescing blood

Your pulse just subtly raised

Not like a storm
Not like a quake

Just like a breeze

You came up to me

I saw the twirling hair
Wide eyes
The groping palms

My arms are open wide

# Deseo

El deseo de cercanía
Crece por la cercanía

El deseo de hablar
Crece hablando

El deseo de ser amado
No se asegura por la respuesta

El deseo de ver lo bello
No se cumple por lo bello

El deseo de dar duración
A este movimiento, a esta conmoción
Es grande, nunca seguro y nunca cumplido

El movimiento permanente
Puede ser amistad
La amistad podría ser
Tan sólo movimiento

Amistad contigo
Con tu misterio
Con tu vulnerabilidad

Es más

# Desire

The desire for closeness
Grows with the closeness

The desire to talk
Grows while talking

The desire to be loved
Is not assured by the answer

The desire to see the beauty
Is not fulfilled by the beauty

The desire to give duration
To this movement, this commotion
Is big, never assured and never fulfilled

Permanent movement
May be friendship
Friendship could be
Simply movement

Friendship with you
With your mystery
With your vulnerability

Is more

# Et altera pars

Il y avait des réalités décevantes
Il y avait des rêves
Il y avait l'envie
Et il y avait le doute

J'étais déchiré
L'amour me prenait des deux côtés

Puis il y a eu l'entretien
Et j'ai perdu une amante
Mais gagné une amie

# The Other Side

There were deceiving realities
There were dreams
There was yearning
And there was doubt


I was disrupted
Love grabbed me from both sides


Then there was conversation
And I lost a lover
But won a friend

# Borderland

At the borderline
Of our friendship
The country of Habibistan begins


There is no barbed wire
But crossing the border
One can be severely
Injured


The passage
Is not mined
But sharply
Guarded


And separately only
Can we pass over
Each one alone
Gets there sometimes
The two of us together
Will not obtain a pass

At times merely
The sentinel will look aside


Then our hands can
Touch
The ground of Habibistan
Imagine
The wideness of the plains
Sense
The summer of the countryside
Feel
The breath of wind

# That Morning When I Left

That morning when I left

There were poems in the air

Pure tender structures made of glass crystals

That would not tolerate

A kitschy glance


What empty talk about

"Togetherness", "Moonshine" or "Lovers' Night"


Two bodies – humans – beings

Who touch each other

Gently, soundlessly

Immersed

In pure existence

And in tenderness

And do not waste
An empty word
About themselves
Or to themselves

And who perceive in profound solidarity and silence
This little rest of life that may remain
Who can only guess and feel themselves

In that tremendous darkness

# Excessive Dreamdefiant Exaggeration

Even though clock hands turn

Theory of relativity yet teaches

That the starry sky

Over there, up there

Above the mist of the Ganges

Can breathlessly stand still

If a grain of sand

Under four eyes

Gets into the gearbox

# Mea Maxima Culpa

At the construction site

Of my inner life

You began

To move rubble out of the way

You stirred the mortar

Carefully poured foundations

And raised the walls

Before the roof

Yet could be shingled

You realized

That I would not

Let you

Live in it

# Storming Brain With Dictionary

| | |
|---|---|
| blindly | being |
| discreetly | bubbly |
| frankly | cozy |
| illiciltely | enamored |
| immoderately | floating |
| improperly | happy |
| inadmissably | kind |
| inexplicably | present |
| outrageously | relaxed |
| shamlessly | satisfied |
| unaskedly | sweet |
| unbelievably | taciturn |
| unbiasedly | tender |
| uncontrollably | timeless |
| unexpectedly | twosome |
| unfoundedly | |
| unimaginably | |
| unintentionally | |
| unpredictably | |
| unpredictably | |
| unrestrictedly | |
| untouchably | |

# Vertigo

Without safety net
Gentle feelings balance
Far afield on the rope

Seldom will they arrive
Without dizziness

# Land, Waste

On the moss at the walls
Of the ruins
A spot
Where something blossoms out

Above the debris field
Light like from Dalí

A whiff of warm breath
Over the plain
Awakes a new remembrance's
Sprout of the potential

Through moss and wild herbs
Between fern and daisies
In a niche
Gentle and soundless
Emerges
A ray

# A Night's Speech

A night's speech
Given by the star
That will lose its manuscript
In daytime


Lovers are the listeners
And they wait until it talks


Music of the spheres
Following the ample score
That man has never seen


The poem's at its end already
And the night
Off goes the alarm clock


Stars are hidden
In the morning light

# Negations

No excessive talk

No reflection

No loving


Letting it come

Letting time work for oneself

Or against oneself


No regretting

No looking forward


Not too intensely, anyway


No arranging

No pushing

No crying


Not too much, anyway

Each one is one
And one is none


No intimidating
No too much, anyway

# Dreamless

As soon as tears become inevitable

You said

As soon as nights begin

To be sleepless

You said

We simply stop


When we began

To retain tears

We long-since were swallowing

Sleeping pills


Meanwhile tears

Have become senseless

And we sleep


Without dreams

# About the Memory of Soul

You may

Destroy the paper

On which they are written

Have thus the feelings

Themselves

Been destroyed?

Even if soul

Is in exile

Does it thus lose

Its memory?

You stay responsible

Of the fox that you once tamed

And the rose that you once tended

Remains unique

Even far away

# Balancing Act

Upright on the rope
For the first time
Being able to look down
Left side and right side
Without getting dizzy

How many steps yet to come?
It would be fine
If the rope
Were unending

Solid ropes could last perhaps
Twenty, thirty years

Or forever

## Assistance

Come to my chest
And cry


And when you are done
We switch sides


And as soon as the both of us
Have been crying enough
Come again to my chest


And we laugh

# Da Capo

Going

Through everything

In memory once more


Listening

To the songs one more time


Writing

The poems anew


Putting

A verb into past tense here


Cutting

A sentence there

Leaving behind
A word

Perceiving
A new tone

Feeling
Hope again

Anticipating
Disaster

Da capo!
Again!

Al segno?
Until the sign?

# Nos acercamos así

Como si nos hubiéramos conocido
Desde hace mucho
Me preguntaste si era él
Del que conocías ya el nombre
Por mi libro
Y empezamos
A hablar de cosas comunes
Sintiendo ya
Que en realidad
Hablamos
De algún amor
Fugitivo
Sin perspectivas
Pero existente
Durante una semana
Sabíamos
Que habíamos
Pasado la límite
De ser extranjeros
El uno para el otro

# The Way We Approached

As if we had known each other

For a long time

You asked if it was me

Whose name you yet knew

From this crazy book

And we began talking

About things of no concern

Feeling already that

In reality

We spoke about love

Just any love

A fugitive love

Without perspective

But existing

During one week

We knew

We had crossed the line

And were no more strangers

# What Will You Do?

What will you do

If after many years

You cross my way by chance?

Will you stop just before

Keep calm and think:

Hey, don't I know this guy?

What was his name?

That must have been in nineteen hundred…

Will you, some little tears in your brown eyes,

Just simply walk ahead

As if you had not seen me?

Or will you joyously

Approach me shouting:

Hey guy, how marvelous to meet you?

And proudly talk about your children,

Home, garden and your part-time job?

Will you, in vaguely trembling voice,
Report on your divorce
– Two years already now ago – ?

And tell me that you surely
Won't fall into the trap again?

Maybe you'll only say:
Hi there – old guy
And slightly nudge my sleeve
We'll have a coffee then
Just like in the old days


What will I do
If after many years
I cross your way by chance?

# Sin consecuencia

Yo te ví

Tu me viste

Me mirabas

Yo te miraba

Se fijaban nuestras miradas

La una en la otra

Tu ardías

Yo ardía

Y voluntarios

No nos tocamos

Ni nos hablamos

Nos separamos

El uno se fué en una dirección

El otro en la otra

# Without Consequence

I saw you

You saw me

You looked at me

I looked at you

Our views entangled

One in the other

You were burning

I was burning

And voluntarily

We did not touch each other

Nor addressed each other

We separated

One went in one direction

The other in the other one

# Omissions

A hand

Not held

Tresses

Not glided over

Lips

That do not touch a cheek

Arms

That do not brush against each other

Glances

That do not meet


Why actually not?


Dreams are not condemnable

# Complicated Constructions

Being allowed to believe
Not to have said anything wrong


Supposing to have been permitted
To have said something wrong


Knowing
That having said something wrong
Does not exclude
Having been


Well understood

# Don't Be a Frog

Why are you so stupid
Little frog?
You hide here in my house
So I can't find you anywhere
Occasionally you beep
Which sucks

Yet maybe you're like me
My brother in spirit, or what?
Scarcely a thumb long is your body
You don't want to show yourself
But make much of a bang

Do you wish to tell me
How insignificant things are?
Just a mosquito here and there
Seems to satisfy your life

Well – your scream for love
I fully understand it

Give me a chance and show yourself
So I can put you into open air
Some day, perhaps your cry
Will then be answered

# When I Invented the Wheel

When I invented the wheel

The very next day

A man from the Patent Cave

Came along and told me

That he already knew

A prospective buyer:

The "International Troglodytes Company"


On the very same evening

I was going to burn my wheel


But I had to realize

That in the meantime

Some idiot

Had invented the

Fire department

# When I Invented then the Powder

When I invented then the powder

I felt quite like a genius

What a joy for people

At holidays be they

National or international

At New Year's Eve, too

When the rockets sprayed

Gold and silver

As well as any color

Against the screen of sky

But then came Brother Schwarz

Invented different designated uses

And I could not

Get my invention undone

# When I Invented then the Rainbow

This happened involuntarily, unexpectedly

Just by the way, at the bank of my river

From under-red to over-purple

It sprawled cone-shaped

From water level up to sky

Where in a nimbostratus it got lost

And many people saw this appearance

Enjoying it quite happily

Jimmy alone did not go there

For rainbows cannot be exploited

As marketable goods or military stuff

For stock exchange they are too volatile

And no one can have rights reserved

This time I felt sincerely happy

And my inventive genius began

To turn to similar phenomena

# Infringing the Provisions

I would like to
Walk on the grass
Pick flowers everywhere
Let my parents, if required
Be liable for me

Exceed speed, ignore red lights
Drive backwards on all of Fifth Avenue

Screw screws in with a hammer
Play drums excessively at three a.m.
Let my dog shit
In the middle of the sidewalk
Drink tea during coffee break
Walk barefoot into Macy's
Call you loudly from the quiet zone
Caress you indecently

I would simply like
To infringe the provisions

# Morpheus' Brother

The priest was talking about dying
The grace of God, eternal life
During more than half an hour
No one was listening to him
The dead man lay there in his coffin
In his grave almost
Why praise him any longer?
He finally has got his peace

The dead ones become more and more
There is no need to care for them
We need you more, my reverend
We who are still living
Though we are in minority
Minorities need to be paid attention to

The priest talked about Lazarus
Does he hope to skirt the constraint of majority?

Oh Pastor, do not be mistaken
You are my brother


Life was not given to me as a fief
It was imposed to me by force
Now tell me, Priest, which is the sense?
Forced to live
Forced to die
Is this the destiny of man?


The priest stopped talking
Shut the bible, sang a chant
– Almost alone –
Shook our hands
Infecting everyone


With Death

# Seems That's the Way I Am

A bit of carefreeness

A bit of earnestness

A bit of Christian social ethics

A bit of freedom reading Sartre

Some absurd by Camus

Some love

By myself?

A bit of Bach, Beethoven and Ray Charles

But not much Michael Jackson

A bit of organ and piano

And saxo-, sometimes vibraphone

And paper, tons of paper


That is the way I am

It seems

# Curtain

No more explanations

A glance

Tender

Comprehensive

Eyelids lowered

A little more than usual

No handshake

Only fingertips

Against each other

Without pressure

Scarcely touched

No more caresses

A kiss?

No, no pathos

And hesitating fingers

Detach one from the other

# Doubts

Indeed dying

Is no way out

But it would settle things

Once and for all

May others now

Take care of the rest

I did my part

Regrettably I failed

Life has no more things in reserve

I would not have already savored

The certitude which I still need

– And think I do already have

For my mind is made up –

Lies in free will

I can renounce
On new editions of experiences
That I do know definitely

But this now
That I had to encounter you
Precisely you
The dearest one I ever had

Enabled me
To breathe now furthermore

# The Jump

Someday I shall jump off
The train I'm sitting in
Or pull the emergency brake
Just without any obvious reason
Then they will call me to account
But I shall only say:
I didn't anyway feel like travelling to
The place the train is heading for
I even don't want back the fare
Keep it and be glad for it

From now on I shall wander
Beside the tracks
And if I meet a switch
I'll trigger it myself
And won't observe stop signals
Any longer even if
It comes to a collision

# Roundabout

On the Champs-Elysées
Of your life
You drove toward the place of stars

Then you came to the roundabout
There were twelve exits and
Too many reasons to choose one of them

You got into the middle of the circle
And drove around, around, around
Surrounded by chaos
And you didn't dare
To change the lanes

Up to this very day
You drive around the ring
Round round
Still is the tank half-filled

# Bugs

Bugs on the table

Cockroaches in a crack

Ah, what delicious lunch!

Dirty dishes of a week

Await my merciless and greasy hands

Afterwards a cig – Shit!

Hole in carpet

Put a brandy bottle on it

Nothing more to see

Yeah, now dossing down a while

Four o'clock, maybe half past

Just have to see Earnie

Wanted to get me a chick

Earnie not at home

Is in custody

Raped a nun, they say

So I'm seeing Bertie

He's got always

Whiskey in stock

Yet – he's shooting up
Which is really not my style
I come in and he is stoned
Not accessible, High like Noon

Loneliness is holy shit

I hit up a doll, but she says
She knows that pickup line long since
At the corner lackadaisically
A dude pukes on a streetlight
And a dog waters a tree
Then flings itself onto a bitch
Shabby, dirty is the world
Let's hurry home
To my dear little cocoon
Where that brandy bottle stays
And no longer I'm alone

# Tua Maxima Culpa

At the construction site

Of your existence

I began

To stake out the ground

I strictly observed

The building regulations

Before the concrete

Yet could have dried

I understood

That you would not

Let me

Live in it

# Paper

I write

What I want

The world may read everything

There is no censorship

You are not bound to believe everything

Even if many a thing

In fact was alike

Or is

And whether I'm sitting

In a dark dungeon

Or on the veranda

It is still the case:

Paper won't blush

# Commandments of The Past

Thou shouldest have had no other gods before me
*Nah, I hadn't. That bit of alcohol, sex, gambling, music won't count, I guess.*


Thou shouldest not have made wrongful use of the name of the Lord your God
*Goddamn, for fuck's sake why not? Sometimes it was quite useful.*


Thou shouldest have remembered the Sabbath day and kept it holy
*I would have liked to do so. My agenda, however, did not always allow. I often sanctified a working day instead.*


Thou shouldest have honored your father and your mother
*I would have liked to do that. But did my father honor me?*


Thou shouldest not have committed murder

*I surely didn't. I was a conscientious objector, after all. Those few mosquitos won't count.*

Thou shouldest not have committed adultery
*Ahem, I only put out feelers…*

Thou shouldest not have stolen
*These few ideas and quotes? No one will notice. And if anybody does – so what?*

Thou shouldest not have born false witness against your neighbor
*I only did that to protect him – or myself.*

Thou shouldest not have coveted your neighbor's house, wife, or male or female slave, or ox, or donkey, or anything that belongs to your neighbor
*Well, I'd also have liked to drive a Cadillac. His wife was ugly, the handmaid old, the donkey tasteless. And never did I enslave anyone.*

# Who I Would Have Loved to Be

Lionel Hampton

Henry Miller

T.S. Eliot

Humphrey Bogart

Mahatma Gandhi

Man on the moon

Groucho Marx

**But not:**

Alfred Nobel

Gollum

The man in the mask

Coronel Paul Tibbets

Charles Manson

Alois Hitler Jr.

Only pipe dreams

I am I

And that will do

# What I Would Have Liked to Be

Gardener of Eden

Doorman of a hen house

Sports reporter of turtle races

Terrorist with ice cream bombs

Indecision-maker

Overcomer

Goer with the wind

Taxi inspector

Architect of cloud-cuckoo-lands

Goat beard barber

Long distance Bobby car race driver

Auxiliary verb policeman

Toy gun runner

Bestselling seller

Global player on words

Andsoonandsoforth


What isn't yet may well still be

# Two-Class Society

Poor or rich

Top and bottom

Weak or strong

Young and old

Social benefits or dividends and bonuses

Wood class or private jet

Full or hungry

Bronx or Beverly Hills

Nonswimmer or lifeguard

Vaccinated or not

Influencer or influenza

Vegan or carnivore

Knavess or knightess

Author/ess or reader/ess


But two-class fe- or male

Are no longer hip

In a queer society

# City Trips

Three miles to go until Harrisburg
Heading for Chernobyl and Fukushima
From Seveso to Bophal
From Stalingrad to Dien Bien Phu
And Saigon to Kabul
From Dachau until Auschwitz
From Lockerbie to Manhattan
Pompeii towards Eyjafjöll
Atlantis to Neapolis
From Vichy to Paris
And Paris unto Moscow
From Berlin 53 to Budapest 56 until Prague 68
From Haskell County to Wuhan

There were and are so many destinations
And be prepared: There will be more

# Notes for a Speech to Graduates

We taught you
That our culture is based
On societies of slaveholders

The best way to resolve conflicts:
Holding the grade book in your hand

That law is defined
By those who got the power

That relations between people
Are described using war metaphors

We taught you
The meaning of humanism
But we forgot to tell you
What it means to be human

# Rhetorical Questions

Where, if not here

How, if not exactly like this

What, if not precisely that

Why, if not for that very reason

To whom, if not to them

Whose, if not ours

Who, if not you and me


When, if not now more than never

?

# Lifted Out of Time

And some day
I shall stand there
In an ornamentless pot
Light as a feather, as grey dust

Don't strew me in the wind
But rather in my river
Which carries me
By its mild drift
Until its end
And pours me out into the sea
Where I shall merge with the grand All

And with You
When Your time comes
And You are lifted
Out of it

# Reading Certain Texts

Reading certain texts
Written by
Eliot, Pound or Yeats
Goethe, Lorca, Baudelaire
Poe and all those Grands

You get the feeling you need not
Write them once again
And you won't anyway
Because pure imitation never works
Yet empathizing, inspiration are permitted
To create something new

Where you, dear reader
On your part feel empathized or inspirited
I reached my goal

# Citations

"The metaphysical error of making an absolute being of one's truelove is paid by poems."
(Octavio Paz)

"Language is the source of misunderstandings."
(Antoine de Saint-Exupéry)

"When – if not now? When should one live if not in the time that is given to us?"
(Christa Wolf)

"Goethe was super. He knew how to rhyme."
(Rudi Carrell)

# Postfarce

Tired I am

Go to my bed

But cannot close an eye

Reader, let your eyes regard

My little book

With favor

*(Inspired by a German children's song)*

# About the Author

Hartmut Aufderstraße

Born in the German countryside of East Westphalia

25 days after Stalin's death

3 months and 18 days before the rebellion in Eastern Germany

Right on the day:

109 years after the birth of Paul Verlaine

100 years after the birth of Vincent van Gogh

74 years after the birth of Albert Einstein

70 years after the death of Karl Marx

20 years after the birth of Michael Caine

8 years after the birth of Eric Clapton

Studies of French, Spanish and Literature at the universities of Bochum and Bielefeld

Teacher in Germany and at the European School of Luxembourg

Author and co-author of numerous textbooks, especially for German as a foreign language

Free lancing author since 1996

Living in South-west-France (Périgord)

Married, 2 sons, 1 grandson (so far)

Fields of interest: Jazz, literature, Bordeaux-wines

Most of the texts published in this book were originally composed in German, some in Spanish or French. Their English versions are not mere translations – which are not imaginable in poetry. They have thus been recreated by the author.

www.aufderstrasse.net

books@aufderstrasse.net

# There Is Some Free Space Here

For your own

Ideas

Inspirations

Fantasies

Rhymed or Unrhymed

If you feel stimulated

To write, scrawl, draw something here

This book will actually be yours